HISTORY & GEOGRAPHY 403
DESERT LANDS

Author:
Theresa K. Buskey, B.A., J.D.

Editor:
Alan Christopherson, M.S.

Assistant Editor:
Annette M. Walker, B.S.

Media Credits:
Page 3: © mycola, iStock, Thinkstock; **4:** © raphoto, iStock,Thinkstock; **9:** © Comstock Images, Stockbyte, Thinkstock; **11:** © Dorling Kindersley, Thinkstock; **12:** © Goodshoot, Thinkstock; **17:** © muha04, iStock,Thinkstock; **23:** © StevenLove, iStock, Thinkstock; twildlife,iStock, Thinkstock; SteveByland, iStock, Thinkstock; estivillml, iStock, Thinkstock; **25:** © Robyn Mackenzie, iStock,Thinkstock; **26:** © filipefrazao, iStock, Thinkstock; **30:** © Anton Foltin, iStock, Thinkstock; **34:** © ZambeziShark, iStock, Thinkstock; **35:** © SumikoPhoto, iStock, Thinkstock; **37:** © heckepics, iStock, Thinkstock; **38:** © cosmopol, iStock, Thinkstock; **41:** © jejim, iStock, Thinkstock; **42:** © Jason Maehl, Hemera, Thinkstock; **44:** © egdigital, iStock, Thinkstock.

Alpha Omega
PUBLICATIONS

804 N. 2nd Ave. E.
Rock Rapids, IA 51246-1759

HISTORY & GEOGRAPHY

STUDENT BOOK

▶ **4th Grade** | Unit 3

Alpha Omega
PUBLICATIONS

DESERT LANDS

Deserts are very dry places. They are found all over the world. In this LIFEPAC® you will learn to find the world's deserts on a map. You will learn about the animals and plants that live in the deserts. You will learn about the minerals that are found there. You will also study some of the peoples who live in the desert. Life is hard in the desert, and you will learn why.

Objectives

Read these objectives. The objectives tell you what you will be able to do when you have successfully completed this LIFEPAC. Each section will list according to the numbers below what objectives will be met in that section. When you have finished this LIFEPAC, you should be able to:

1. Locate seven of the great deserts of the world on a map.
2. Know the continents and some map features.
3. Explain how moisture is blocked from reaching a desert.
4. Explain how plants and animals live in the desert.
5. Describe seven of the major deserts of the world.
6. Describe the traditional ways of life in the desert.
7. Know the names and locations of some desert people.
8. Explain how modern inventions help people to live in the desert.

1. WHAT IS A DESERT?

A desert is a place where very little rain falls and very few plants grow. Most deserts are very hot, too. Very few plants and animals can live in a desert because of the heat and lack of food.

Even in the desert, however, God has created life. Special plants and animals can live in the hot, dry deserts of the world. People, also, have learned how to live in the desert. They use the plants and animals God put there to help them survive.

Objectives

Review these objectives. When you have completed this section, you should be able to:

2. Know the continents and some map features.
3. Explain how moisture is blocked from reaching a desert.
4. Explain how plants and animals live in the desert.

Vocabulary

Study these new words. Learning the meanings of these words is a good study habit and will improve your understanding of this LIFEPAC.

barren (bar ən). Not able to produce much.

burrow (bėr′ ō). A hole in the ground used by an animal for shelter.

cactus (kak′ təs). A fleshy plant with spines instead of leaves that grows in hot, dry regions of America.

dew (dü). Moisture from the air that collects on cool surfaces at night.

domesticate (də mes′ tə kā t). To make a wild animal tame.

dune (dün). A hill of sand heaped up by the wind.

evaporate (i vap′ ə rāt). To change from a liquid into a gas.

fog (fog). Thick mist.

hibernate (hī' bər nāt). To spend part of the year sleeping, or dormant.

moisture (mois' chər). Water spread in very small drops in the air or on a surface.

preserve (pri zėrv'). To prepare food to keep it from spoiling.

rodent (rōd' nt). Any of a group of animals with large front teeth that are used for gnawing. Includes rats, mice, and squirrels.

Tropic of Cancer (trop' ik   uv   kan'sər). An imaginary line north of the equator that marks the northern boundary of the tropical zone.

Tropic of Capricorn (trop' ik   uv   kap' rə kôrn). An imaginary line south of the equator that marks the southern boundary of the tropical zone.

Note: *All vocabulary words in this LIFEPAC appear in* **boldface** *print the first time they are used. If you are unsure of the meaning when you are reading, study the definitions given.*

Pronunciation Key: h**a**t, **ā**ge, c**ã**re, f**ä**r; l**e**t, **ē**qual, t**ė**rm; **i**t, **ī**ce; h**o**t, **ō**pen, **ô**rder; **oi**l; **ou**t; c**u**p, p**u̇**t, r**ü**le; **ch**ild; lo**ng**; **th**in; /ᵀH/ for **th**en; /zh/ for mea**s**ure; /u/ or /ə/ represents /a/ in **a**bout, /e/ in tak**e**n, /i/ in penc**i**l, /o/ in lem**o**n, and /u/ in circ**u**s.

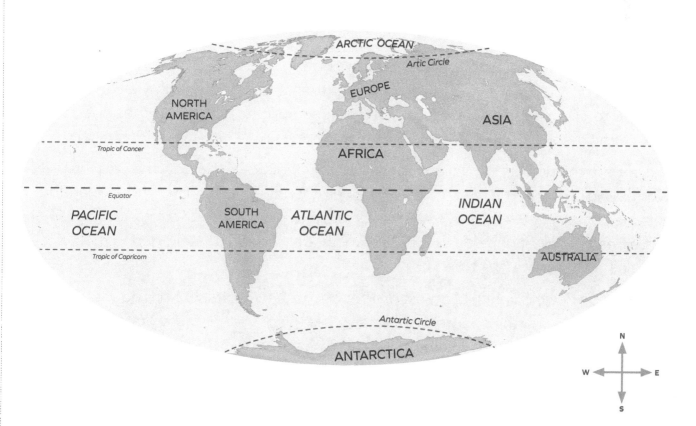

 Map hint: The easiest way to learn directions is to remember that when you face north, south is behind you, east is towards your right hand, and west is toward your left. This works for east and west when you are looking at a map with north at the top, also.

Use the map to answer the following questions.

Answer each with north, south, east, or west.

1.1   Antarctica is _____ of Africa.

1.2   The Pacific Ocean is on the _____ side of North America.

1.3   The Tropic of Cancer is _____ of the Equator.

1.4   Asia is _____ of Europe.

1.5   The Tropic of Capricorn is _____ of Asia.

1.6   The Indian Ocean is on the _____ side of Africa's Hemisphere.

Description of Deserts

Scientists usually call a place a desert if it only gets 10 inches (25 centimeters) or less of rain in a year. Most places get much more rain than that. For example, Chicago, Illinois gets 20 to 40 inches of rain a year, and New York City gets 40 to 60 inches a year. This lack of rain means there is very little **moisture** in a desert.

Moisture in the air acts like a blanket. It keeps the heat out in the daytime and the warm air in at night. The desert, however, does not have a moisture blanket. Therefore, deserts get very hot in the daytime and very cold at night. Deserts often change 25° or more between night and day, so a person might be wearing a T-shirt during the day but need a heavy coat at night.

Deserts can be cold or hot, but most are hot because they are near the equator. On our earth, things nearer the equator are hotter, while things further away are cooler. The North and South Poles are cold because they are as far away from the equator as it is possible to be.

Deserts form when something stops moisture from reaching that place. Moisture is carried by clouds. Usually mountains stop the clouds from bringing their rain to the desert. Also, as air moves around the earth it tends to create areas of high and low rainfall. The biggest areas of low rain are along the line of the **Tropic of Cancer**, north of the equator and the **Tropic of Capricorn**, south of the equator.

(Remember: Capricorn is a bigger word and sinks to the bottom, or south).

① Water evaporates from the ocean...

② ...forming clouds that are blown to the mountains...

③ ...where the rain empties back into the ocean.

Meanwhile, the desert remains dry, with little or no moisture.

| Mountains can cause deserts.

Moisture gets into a cloud when it **evaporates** from a big lake or ocean. The wind blows the clouds toward the mountains. The clouds have to go up and over the mountains to reach the desert on the other side, but the moisture in the clouds falls out as it gets cooler going up the mountain. Thus, by the time the clouds get to the other side of the mountain there is very little moisture left. In fact, often there is no cloud left at all. The desert is the *rain shadow* of the mountain.

Without any moisture, very few plants can grow in the desert. Plants keep soil from being blown or washed away, so deserts are often covered with loose sand or rocks because much of the soil has been blown away. Strong winds can cause dust or sand storms that block out the sun and make it hard to see or breathe. Sometimes the sand can be blown into big piles like snowdrifts. These are called **dunes**.

Put the correct word on each line.

1.7 Very little rain falls along the Tropic of _____ or the

Tropic of _____ .

1.8 A desert usually receives _____ or less inches of rain in a year.

1.9 Deserts are often covered with loose sand or _____ .

1.10 Deserts are often found behind mountains in the mountains'

_____ .

1.11 Very few animals can live in a desert because of the heat and lack of

_____ .

1.12 Moisture in the air acts like a _____ , keeping heat in at night.

Life in the Desert

People and animals can live in the desert if there are enough plants. Some parts of the desert get only one inch of rain in a year. No plants grow there, and almost nothing else can live there. Other parts of the desert get enough rain for special desert plants to grow. People and animals can use these plants to survive.

Desert plants. God created very special plants that can live in a desert. These plants were created to use the little moisture of the desert very carefully, so most deserts are not big, empty piles of sand. Usually there are plants, often many plants. They grow far apart so they don't have to share any moisture.

God thought of many ways to help plants survive in the desert. All plants collect water through their roots. Some desert plants have roots that spread way out to get all the water they can when it rains. Other plants put down very deep roots to reach water under the ground. Some plants have leaves that collect **fog** or **dew** and drop the moisture for their roots to get. Other plants grow from seeds only when it rains. They grow, produce seeds, and die quickly. Their seeds will not grow until the next rain.

The desert plant most people know about is the **cactus**. They are found in the deserts of North and South America. A cactus does not have leaves like a tree because moisture evaporates from leaves. Instead, cacti are covered with a waxy coating that keeps moisture inside. The inside of a cactus is like a big sponge. When it does rain, the cactus soaks up the water and stores it to use when it is dry. The cactus is covered with sharp spines or needles to keep animals from getting the water inside.

There are many kinds of cacti. The saguaro may grow to be 60 feet (18 meters) tall and has arms that make it look like a person being held up by a robber. The prickly pear cactus grows small, paddle-shaped arms and a pear-shaped fruit that is good to eat. The barrel cactus is shaped like a barrel and covered with hard, curved spikes. Cacti grow beautiful flowers for a very short time when there is enough rain.

| Cactus

The mesquite is another desert plant. It is a small tree which sends its roots deep into the soil to collect every bit of water it can find. It has small, waxy leaves that do not lose much moisture. Some animals can eat the leaves. People can use the wood for fuel and to build things. They also grind the mesquite beans into flour to use for food.

Another useful desert plant is the date palm. It grows in the deserts of northern Africa and western Asia. Date palms grow near a source of water called an **oasis**. They can be used for food, shade, and fuel for fires.

Dates are the food grown by the palm trees. They are a very sweet fruit. They are easy to dry and **preserve**. They can be pressed into cakes which are easy for travelers to carry. Dates are an important source of food for the desert people.

People can also use other parts of the date palm. The leaves can be used to make baskets or mats. Rope can be made from the bark. The tree can be used to build shelters. Even the pits from the dates can be used as fuel for a fire or food for animals.

God cleverly made many plants that can grow in the desert by making good use of the little moisture there. Thus, God provides for men and animals even in the driest places.

Match these words with the correct description.

1.13	_____ cactus	a.	make baskets or mats
1.14	_____ mesquite	b.	puts down deep roots
1.15	_____ date	c.	sweet fruit
1.16	_____ palm leaves	d.	inside like a sponge

Name four ways God made plants able to live in a desert.

1.17   a. _____

   b. _____

   c. _____

   d. _____

Complete this activity.

See if someone in your class can bring in some dates for the class to eat. Discuss the taste. Talk about what it would be like to eat dates every day.

Desert animals. Many wild animals make their homes in the desert. God created these animals especially to live in the desert. Most of these animals are small. They are small so they do not need much food and they can easily find shade from the sun. Most of the animals hide in a **burrow** or under rocks and shrubs during the daytime. They come out to find food at night when it is cooler. There are fewer animals in a desert because there is less food for them to eat.

Desert animals can go without water for days. Some, like the kangaroo rat, do not need to drink water at all. They get all the moisture they need from the food they eat.

Desert animals have many ways to live in their harsh home. The sandgrouse, an African desert bird, can soak up water in its feathers to bring to its babies in the nest. Desert hares have large ears that take extra heat away from their bodies. A desert chameleon in Africa turns white in the hottest part of the day, to reflect sunlight away. A tortoise in Asia is active only a few months of the year, when the rain has made the desert green. The rest of the year it **hibernates** underground. Many bigger animals, like antelope and gazelles, live by traveling around constantly to search for food.

Desert animals eat many kinds of things. The kangaroo rat lives on seeds and plants. The horned lizard eats insects. The rattlesnake and the coyote hunt small **rodents** and rabbits that live in the desert. So, there is food in the desert. It is just hard to find.

| Desert animals that live in or above burrows

The most useful desert animal is the camel. The camel is a **domesticated** animal that comes from Africa and Asia. People use them to carry heavy loads across the desert. The camel was created by God to survive in the desert.

| Person riding a camel near the Great Pyramids, Egypt

Camels have wide hoofs that allow them to walk on top of sand. Their nostrils are small slits which can be closed to keep out sand during a storm. They also have extra eyelids, and hair covering their ears, to keep out the sand. They have big humps on their backs which store fat, so they can go many days without eating. They do not need much water, either, because they can get moisture from the food they eat, and they do not lose much moisture by sweating. The camel can also store a lot of water in its stomach.

Desert people used the camel for food. They ate its meat and drank its milk. Its hide and hair were used for clothes, blankets, and leather goods.

Camels can carry heavy loads of up to 400 pounds (180 kilograms), but they do not like to work. They will bite, kick, or spit at people when they are mad, but desert people needed and used them anyway. The camel is called the "ship of the desert," because it carries things back and forth across the desert as ships do on the sea. The camel was a very useful animal for people who lived in the desert before the invention of cars and trucks. Even today, camels can cross deserts without the roads trucks need. Then again, the trucks do not bite!

Match these words with the correct description.

1.18 _____ kangaroo rat

1.19 _____ camel

1.20 _____ antelope

1.21 _____ horned lizard

1.22 _____ sandgrouse

1.23 _____ coyote

a. eats insects

b. carries water to the nest in its feathers

c. drinks no water, eats seeds

d. domesticated

e. moves around constantly to search for food

f. eats rodents and rabbits

List some of the things that make the camel the "ship of the desert."

1.24 a. _____

b. _____

c. _____

d. _____

Complete this activity.

1.25 Find a book about deserts and choose a desert animal from it (not a camel). Write a report on that animal.

> **Teacher check:**
>
> Initials _____ Date _____

Review the material in this section to prepare for the Self Test. The Self Test will check your understanding of this section. Any items you miss on this test will show you what areas you will need to restudy in order to prepare for the unit test.

SELF TEST 1

Answer *true* or *false* (1 point each answer).

1.01 _____ Camels are gentle animals, easy to work with.

1.02 _____ Desert hares have large ears that carry away heat from their bodies.

1.03 _____ Cacti are covered with poison to keep animals from eating them.

1.04 _____ Some desert plants grow and produce seeds quickly after a rain.

1.05 _____ Strong winds in the desert cause dust or sand storms.

1.06 _____ Deserts are always hot.

1.07 _____ Desert plants are just like plants in wetter places.

1.08 _____ Food is hard to find in the desert.

1.09 _____ Desert plants do not produce food people can eat.

1.010 _____ Desert people ate camel meat.

Match these items (2 points each answer).

1.011 _____ cactus   a. eats rodents and rabbits

1.012 _____ date palm   b. moves to find food

1.013 _____ kangaroo rat   c. has an inside like a sponge

1.014 _____ oasis   d. to change from liquid to gas

1.015 _____ antelope   e. a hill of sand piled up by the wind

1.016 _____ mesquite   f. produces fruit and leaves for mats

1.017 _____ dune   g. eats seeds, does not need water

1.018 _____ burrow   h. hole in the ground, animal's home

1.019 _____ rattlesnake   i. small desert tree with deep roots

1.020 _____ evaporate   j. a green place in the desert where there is water

Choose the correct word to complete each sentence (3 points each answer).

roots	Cancer	Capricorn	fog
Equator	saguaro	rocks	blanket
prickly pear	moisture	mesquite	

1.021 The line of low rainfall north of the equator is the Tropic of

_____ .

1.022 The line of low rainfall south of the equator is the Tropic of

_____ .

1.023 Name two kinds of cactus: _____ and

_____ .

1.024 Moisture in the air acts like a _____ to keep a

place warmer at night.

1.025 Places on earth are hotter as you get closer to the _____ and

cooler as you get further away.

1.026 Deserts are covered with loose sand or _____ .

1.027 Some desert plants collect _____ on their leaves,

which drops to their roots.

1.028 Deserts form when something stops _____

from reaching that place.

1.029 Desert plants sometimes have deep or spread out _____

to find water.

Answer each question (5 points each answer).

1.030   What does it mean to say that a desert is in the rain shadow of a mountain?

_____

_____

_____

_____

1.031   Name three ways the camel was created by God to be the "ship of the desert."

a. _____

b. _____

c. _____

1.032   What is a desert?

_____

_____

1.033   What is there for animals to eat in the desert?

a. _____

b. _____

c. _____

✔ **Teacher check:**   Initials   _____   **80**

Score _____   Date   _____   **100**

2. WHERE ARE THE DESERTS?

Deserts exist all over the world. Europe is the only continent that does not have a desert. The map below shows the important deserts of the world.

In this section you will learn about these deserts. You will learn where they are, why they are deserts, and what they are like. Each desert is unique, just as each person is unique. Our wonderful God never makes anything in his creation the same way twice.

Objectives

Review these objectives. When you have completed this section, you should be able to:

1. Locate seven of the great deserts of the world on a map.
2. Know the continents and some map features.
3. Explain how moisture is blocked from reaching a desert.
5. Describe seven of the major deserts of the world.

Vocabulary

Study these new words. Learning the meanings of these words is a good study habit and will improve your understanding of this LIFEPAC.

Arabian Peninsula (ə rā′ bē ən pe nin′ sə lə). A piece of land in southwest Asia surrounded by the Red Sea, the Indian Ocean, and the Persian Gulf.

altitude (al′ tə tüd). Height above the level of the ocean.

barren (bar ən). Not able to produce much.

coast (kō st). The land along the sea.

continent (kon′ tə nənt). One of the seven great masses of land on earth. (North America, South America, Africa, Europe, Asia, Australia, Antarctica)

continuous (kən tin′ yü əs). Without a stop or break.

export (ek spôrt'). To send goods out of one country for sale and use in another.

fertilizer (fėr' təl ī zė r). A substance put into or on the soil to make it produce more.

gorge (gôrj). A deep, narrow valley, usually steep and rocky.

lava (lä' və). The hot, melted rock that flows out of a volcano.

livestock (lī v' stok). Farm animals.

mineral (min' ər əl). Anything that is not a plant, animal, or other living thing. Usually a valuable rock or liquid taken from the earth.

plain (plān). A flat stretch of land.

riverbed (riv' ər bed'). The channel in which a river flows.

Sahel (sä hel'). An area south of the Sahara Desert that has periods without enough rain for crops and pasture.

scenery (sə' nər ē). The general appearance of a place.

surround (sə round'). To be on all sides of; enclose.

unique (yü nēk'). Being the only one of its kind.

Pronunciation Key: h**a**t, **ā**ge, c**ã**re, f**ä**r; l**e**t, **ē**qual, t**ė**rm; **i**t, **ī**ce; h**o**t, **ō**pen, **ô**rder; **oi**l; **ou**t; c**u**p, p**u̇**t, r**ü**le; **ch**ild; lo**ng**; **th**in; /ͳH/ for **th**en; /zh/ for mea**s**ure; /u/ or /ə/ represents /a/ in **a**bout, /e/ in tak**e**n, /i/ in penc**i**l, /o/ in lem**o**n, and /u/ in circ**u**s.

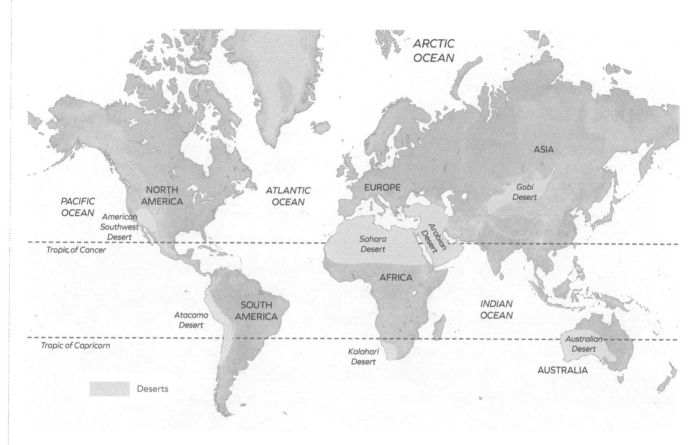

| Seven of the World's Great Deserts

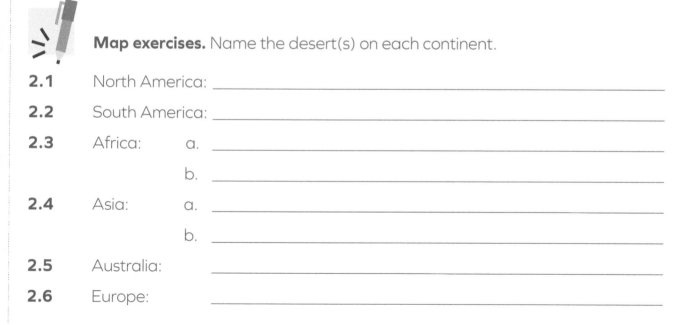

Map exercises. Name the desert(s) on each continent.

2.1 North America: _____

2.2 South America: _____

2.3 Africa: a. _____

                 b. _____

2.4 Asia: a. _____

                 b. _____

2.5 Australia: _____

2.6 Europe: _____

Deserts of the Northern Hemisphere

The Sahara Desert. The Sahara Desert of North Africa is the world's largest desert. It is almost the same size as the United States. The Sahara touches ten different countries in Africa. The name, *Sahara*, comes from the Arabic word for desert.

The Atlas Mountains that run along the **coast** of Africa stop moisture from reaching the Sahara. Most of the desert is covered with bare gravel or sand dunes. There is very little water anywhere. The Nile River flows through the desert, and there are some oases scattered over the desert. These are the only places people can grow food.

The area along the bottom (southern) edge of the Sahara is called the **Sahel**. It is a very dry area, though not quite as dry as the Sahara. The Sahara is getting bigger each year however, and more Sahel is becoming Sahara.

Oil has been found under some countries in the desert. This is pumped up and sold to make money for those countries. Most of the other countries of the Sahara are very poor because they do not have good land to grow food for people or their **livestock**.

The Arabian Desert. The Arabian Desert is the name used for all of the deserts on the **Arabian Peninsula**. Since most of the real names are Arabic, such as *Al Jafurah* and *Rub' al-Khali*, it is easier for us to refer to it as the Arabian Desert. The Rub' al-Khali (Empty Quarter) is the largest **continuous** area of sand desert in the world.

A long string of mountains runs along the Red Sea blocking any moisture that might reach the desert. Also, the Arabian Desert, like the Sahara, is near the Tropic of Cancer, which makes it a very dry area. There are no rivers in this desert. There are many dry **riverbeds**, called *wadis*. When it does rain, it rains very hard, and the *wadis* fill up with water for a little while.

However, the Arabian Desert is a very rich place. It is rich in oil. The biggest nation in the desert, Saudi Arabia, **exports** more oil than any other nation on earth. The other nations also have large amounts of oil they sell. Many of these countries have become very rich because of the oil under their deserts.

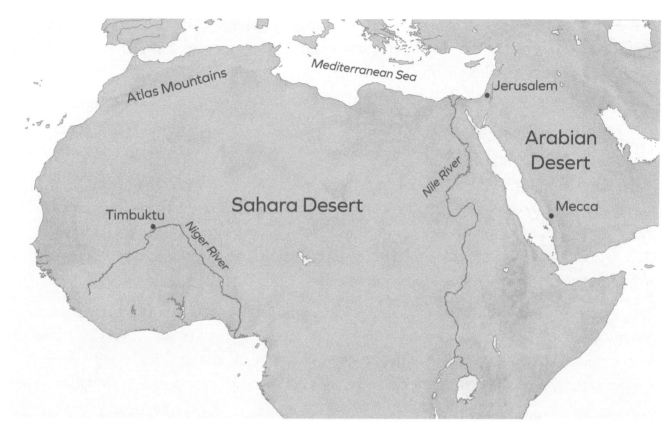

| The Sahara and its neighbors

  Put the correct answer on each line.

2.7   The Arabian Desert is rich in _____ .

2.8   The dry area along the southern edge of the Sahara is called the _____ .

2.9   The _____ Mountains block the moisture of the ocean

         from reaching the Sahara.

2.10   Dry Arabian riverbeds are called _____ .

2.11   The largest continuous area of sand desert in the world is called

         _____ .

2.12   The Arabian and Sahara Deserts are on the Tropic of _____ .

2.13   The _____ is the largest desert in the world.

2.14   The _____ River flows through the Sahara.

The Gobi Desert. The Gobi Desert is in the country of Mongolia in Asia. It is the coldest desert you will study and the furthest north. The Gobi Desert is as far north as New York and Michigan in the United States.

Because it is a desert, it gets very hot in the summer and because it is so far north, it gets very cold in the winter. It can get to 110°F in the summer and 40°F below zero in the winter. That is a change of 150°F from summer to winter!

The Gobi is **surrounded** by mountains on three sides. The mountains block so much moisture that only about eight inches of rain fall in a year. There are a few rivers that flow into the Gobi from the mountains. These often do not flow all year and dry up quickly after they reach the desert. There is some water underground that can be reached by digging wells, but there are no oases in the Gobi.

The center of the desert is the most **barren** place. It is covered with hard packed, stony ground and smaller areas of sand. Around that are dry, grassy **plains** called *steppes*. Animals that eat grass can live on the steppes. The people of the Gobi live by raising livestock on the steppes. These people are called Mongols and you will study them later.

The American Southwest Desert. The desert area of the American Southwest is in the United States and Mexico in North America. This area includes several different deserts that together are called the American Southwest Desert.

A long chain of mountains runs <u>all</u> <u>the</u> <u>way</u> from Alaska to the Antarctic Ocean, along the western sides of North and South America. In the United States and Canada they are the Rocky Mountains. In Mexico, they call them the Sierra Madre Mountains. In South America, they are called the Andes Mountains. Just north of the Tropic of Cancer, the deserts of the American Southwest are located around the Rocky Mountains.

Many of the American deserts are mixed in with the mountains that stop their moisture. This makes for beautiful **scenery** where the colorful mountains rise out of the deserts. The Colorado, or Painted Desert is especially beautiful, because of the different colors of the layers of rock in the mountains. The change in **altitude** can be very great. The Mojave (mō hä' ve) Desert can be as high as 5,000 feet above sea level and goes as low as 492 feet <u>below</u> sea level. That is the lowest spot in North America, called Death Valley.

The Great Basin is the largest desert that is only in the United States. The Great Basin is a group of bowl-like valleys surrounded by mountains. Water that flows into the Great Basin cannot get back out again. The Great Salt Lake in Utah is in the bottom of one of these bowls. It is salty because the water cannot leave. It can only evaporate and leave salt behind, just like the ocean.

Many rivers run through the American Desert. These rivers provide water for men and animals. The rivers often are in a deep **gorge**, like the Grand Canyon around the Colorado River in Arizona. The Colorado River is the biggest river of the American deserts.

Other Northern Deserts. There is also a string of Asian deserts between the Arabian Desert and the Gobi Desert in the Northern Hemisphere. They have very difficult names and you do not have to learn them. There is another desert called the Thar which is along the border between India and Pakistan in Asia.

| Clockwise: Scorpions are commonly found in the desert. Mojave Rattlesnake. Desert Hare. Death Valley, California.

Put the correct word on each line.

2.15   The mountains that run along the west coast of the Americas are called

the _____ in the United States and Canada,

the _____ in Mexico, and the _____

in South America.

2.16   The lowest spot in North America is _____ .

2.17   The grassy plains of the Gobi Desert are called _____ .

2.18   The _____ Desert is along the border between India and Pakistan.

2.19   The Gobi Desert is in the country of _____ .

Answer _true_ or _false_.

2.20   _____   The Gobi Desert is in Europe.

2.21   _____   The Great Salt Lake is salty because the water that comes into it
evaporates and leaves salt behind.

2.22   _____   The rivers that run through the American Desert are often down in
deep gorges.

2.23   _____   The temperature in the Gobi Desert only changes about 30° in a
year.

2.24   _____   The Gobi Desert is further north than the Sahara Desert.

2.25   _____   The center of the Gobi Desert is a big oasis.

2.26   _____   The Colorado River flows through the American Southwest Desert.

Deserts of the Southern Hemisphere

The Kalahari Desert. The Kalahari Desert is in southern Africa right on the Tropic of Capricorn. It covers most of the country of Botswana. It is shaped like a bowl set high up in the mountains that surround it. The mountains block the Kalahari from the ocean on three sides. Only the north, which is toward the rest of Africa, is not blocked by mountains.

Very deep, red sand covers most of the desert. The north and west have large plains where many kinds of plants grow. The desert gets rain when the wind blows from the Indian Ocean bringing moisture.

The plains of the Kalahari get more rain than most deserts. Parts can get as much as 18 inches in a year. It is a desert because there is very little water on top of the ground. You can count on your fingers the water holes that have water all year. When it does rain, the water goes into large, flat areas called pans until it evaporates. These pans are very important sources of water for the animals of the desert.

The Australian Desert. Most of the center part of the nation/continent of Australia is desert. It is right on the Tropic of Capricorn. The center area is called the Outback. Most of it is sandy and barren, but some sparse grasses that are good for sheep grow on the edges. People live on ranches called stations and raise sheep in the Outback.

The moisture that might reach the desert from the Pacific Ocean is stopped by the Great Dividing Range. The Dividing Range is a line of mountains along Australia's east coast.

There are several empty "lakes" in the Australian Desert. They are called *playas*. These fill up with water when there is a time of heavy rain and become genuine lakes for a short time. Fish are washed into the lake, and these attract birds and other animals. Then, the lake dries up, the fish die, and the birds leave—until the next heavy rain, when the cycle begins again. The largest *playa* is named Lake Disappointment. Why is that a good name?

| Outback sheep

| Flamingos in the Atacama Desert

The *playas* and little holes that catch rainwater are the only sources of water on top of the ground. These will all dry up a little while after the rain. The only other place to get water is from wells dug to reach water under the ground.

The Atacama Desert. The Atacama Desert is on the Tropic of Capricorn in Chile, South America. The Atacama is one of the driest places on earth. In some places it may rain less than an inch every <u>ten</u> years. There are very few plants or animals in this desert.

The Atacama is an unusual desert. It is not blocked off from the ocean by mountains. It is in the Andes Mountains right next to the Pacific Ocean! The ocean is the reason it is a desert.

Cold water from Antarctica flows up along the **coast** of South America. The cold water makes the air over the ocean cold, too. That cold air loses its moisture, just the same as it does when it gets cold going up a mountain. Thus, the air that reaches the coast has almost no moisture left, so only fog reaches the coast, not rain.

Several rivers flow into the desert from the mountains. Only one of the rivers, the Loa, reaches the ocean. The other rivers dry up in the desert. There is also water in the rocks and dirt under the desert. This is called the Pica **Aquifer**.

The Atacama is covered with sand, cooled **lava**, and huge salt lakes. The salt lakes are called *salars*. These are large lakes where water has come in, cannot get out, and is

HISTORY & GEOGRAPHY 403

LIFEPAC TEST

NAME _____

DATE _____

SCORE _____

80 / 100

HISTORY & GEOGRAPHY 403: LIFEPAC TEST

Answer *true* or *false* (1 point each answer).

1. _____ Children of the Australian Desert go to school by radio.

2. _____ The cactus stores water in its trunk like a sponge.

3. _____ Deserts are all empty piles of sand.

4. _____ A desert receives 30 or more inches of rain in a year.

5. _____ A desert is often very hot in the day and cold at night.

6. _____ Desert plants die when it rains.

7. _____ The kangaroo rat must live near water so it can get a long drink every day.

8. _____ It has always been easy for people to live in the desert.

9. _____ Hopi and Navajo people made beautiful blankets, baskets, and pottery.

10. _____ Desert lakes are often salty because the water evaporates and leaves salt behind.

11. _____ Places on earth are colder as you get nearer the equator.

Complete these sentences (3 points each answer).

12. The line of dry area south of the equator is along the

    _____ .

13. The line of dry area north of the equator is along the

    _____ .

14. Some nomads earned gold by taking _____ from the mines to Timbuktu across the Sahara.

15. The most important animal to the Mongol nomads was the _____ .

16. The half of the earth north of the equator is called the

    _____ .

17. Name one modern way to bring water into the desert:

_____ .

18. The largest desert in the world is the _____ Desert.

19. The Arabian Desert is rich in _____ .

20. The half of the earth south of the equator is called the

_____ .

21. Traditional desert people who eat what they can kill or find are called

_____ .

22. Most desert animals hunt for food (when?) _____ .

Match these items (2 points each answer).

23. _____ nomad

24. _____ camel

25. _____ livestock

26. _____ date palm

27. _____ hydroponics

28. _____ villagers

29. _____ aquifer

30. _____ solar panels

31. _____ felt

32. _____ oasis

33. _____ pueblo

34. _____ mesquite

a. pressed-down wool cloth

b. large area of underground water

c. "ship of the desert"

d. make electricity from sunlight

e. traditional people who move to find food for their animals

f. farm animals

g. a green place in the desert where there is water

h. desert plant that has fruit, leaves for mats, and bark for ropes

i. Hopi village

j. raising crops without dirt, in a special liquid

k. traditional desert people who grow crops around water

l. desert plant with waxy leaves and deep roots and edible bean pods

Name the continent where each desert is located (3 points each answer).

35. American Southwest _____

36. Atacama _____

37. Sahara _____

38. Kalahari _____

39. Arabian _____

40. Gobi _____

41. Australian _____

42. no deserts at all _____

Answer this question (4 points this answer).

43. How do the people of the Atacama Desert "harvest the clouds"?

_____

_____

_____

_____

Complete this list (2 points each answer).

44. List two ways moisture can be blocked from reaching a desert.

a. _____

b. _____

evaporating away. The salt and other **minerals** left behind change the water to many beautiful colors. *Salars* can be blue, green, gray, and even pink!

The Atacama is rich in minerals. It has more sodium nitrate than any other place on earth. Sodium nitrate is used to make bombs and **fertilizer**. Copper, an important metal, and other minerals are also found in the desert.

Other Southern Deserts. There are two other big deserts in the Southern Hemisphere. The Namib Desert is in southern Africa on the west coast. Its name means "an area where there is nothing." It is on the Tropic of Capricorn. It is a desert for the same reason as the Atacama. The cold ocean current from Antarctica also keeps moisture from reaching this coast, except as fog.

The Patagonian Desert is at the southern end of Argentina on the east side of South America. It is the largest desert in the Americas. It is not on the Tropic of Capricorn. The winds always come from the west, over the Andes Mountains, so all their moisture is gone by the time they reach the desert.

Put the correct word on the line from the list below.

| pans | Andes | Patagonian | *playa* |
| Australian | *salars* | Pica | hemisphere |

2.27 _____ The aquifer under the Atacama Desert.

2.28 _____ Lake Disappointment is the largest.

2.29 _____ Mountains that block moisture from reaching the Patagonian.

2.30 _____ One half of the earth.

2.31 _____ This desert is not on the Tropic of Capricorn.

2.32 _____ This desert is on a continent that is also a country.

2.33 _____ Huge salt lakes in the Atacama Desert.

2.34 _____ Large, flat areas in the Kalahari that collect water after a rain.

Answer each question.

2.35   What stops moisture from reaching the Namib and Atacama Deserts?

_____

_____

_____

_____

2.36   The Kalahari receives more rain than most deserts.
Why is it still called a desert?

_____

_____

Do this crossword puzzle.

2.37   Read the puzzle clues and write the words in the puzzle.

Across

3. the Great Salt Lake is here, largest desert located only in the United States

5. along the border of India and Pakistan

6. North America's deserts are together called the _____ Southwest Desert*

8. a desert rich in oil in southwest Asia that has no rivers, only *wadis**

10. the _____ Desert is on the only continent that is also a country*

11. these mountains block moisture from reaching the Sahara

14. the dry area south of the equator runs along the line of the Tropic of _____

15. The largest area of continuous sand desert in the world

16. The desert of Mongolia which includes *steppes**

Down

1. the lowest point in North America
2. the largest desert in the world, located in North Africa*
4. the dry area north of the equator runs along the line of the Tropic of

   _____

6. the desert on the coast in Chile, South America, created by cold water from Antarctica*
7. the largest desert in the Americas, in Argentina
9. desert of southern Africa, mostly in Botswana*
12. desert of the southwest coast of Africa, caused by the cold water from Antarctica
13. river of the Sahara

*Know these deserts and their locations.

| The Sonoran Desert

Review the material in this section to prepare for the Self Test. The Self Test will check your understanding of this section and will review the other section. Any items you miss on this test will show you what areas you will need to restudy in order to prepare for the unit test.

SELF TEST 2

Answer _true_ or _false_ (1 point each answer).

2.01 _____ Deserts are usually covered with sand or rocks.

2.02 _____ Water only comes into the Great Salt Lake in Utah; it never goes back out.

2.03 _____ Dunes are piles of sand blown by the wind.

2.04 _____ Desert plants are just like plants in wetter places.

2.05 _____ Most desert animals hunt for food when the sun is high so they can see better.

2.06 _____ There are never any rivers in a desert.

2.07 _____ The Sahel is part of the Australian Desert.

2.08 _____ The temperature in a desert is often hot during the day and cool at night.

2.09 _____ Heavy rains can make lakes in the desert for a short period of time.

2.010 _____ A desert usually receives 10 inches or less rain in a year.

2.011 _____ The prickly pear cactus produces an edible fruit.

Put the correct answer on the line (4 points each answer).

2.012 The line of dry area south of the equator is along the

_____ .

2.013 The line of dry area north of the equator is along the

_____ .

2.014 The half of the earth north of the equator is called the

_____ .

2.015 The half of the earth south of the equator is called the

_____ .

Match these items by putting the correct letter on the line (2 points each answer).

2.016 _____ antelope

2.017 _____ cactus

2.018 _____ livestock

2.019 _____ aquifer

2.020 _____ mesquite

2.021 _____ camel

2.022 _____ coyote

2.023 _____ oasis

2.024 _____ date palm

2.025 _____ kangaroo rat

a. eats rodents and rabbits

b. eats seeds, needs no water

c. "ship of the desert"

d. farm animals

e. a green place in the desert where there is water

f. moves constantly to search for food

g. grows fruit, fuel, and leaves for mats

h. inside like a sponge

i. grows deep roots to get water

j. a large area of water under the ground

Choose the correct word to complete each sentence (4 points each answer).

Sahara	Atacama	Kalahari	American Southwest
Arabian	Australian	Gobi	

2.026 The _____ Desert is along the west coast of South America in Chile.

2.027 The _____ , the largest desert in the world, is in North Africa.

2.028 The _____ Desert is in Mongolia, Asia.

2.029 Part of the _____ Desert is in the United States.

2.030 The _____ Desert is in southwest Asia, on a peninsula rich in oil.

2.031 The _____ is on the only continent that is also a country.

2.032 The _____ is in Botswana in southern Africa.

Answer each question (5 points each answer).

2.033 What is the "rain shadow" of a mountain?

_____

_____

_____

2.034 What makes the Namib and the Atacama so dry despite the fact they are on the coast of an ocean?

_____

_____

_____

_____

2.035 Why are lakes found in a desert often salty?

_____

_____

_____

2.036 Name three reasons a camel can live and work in the desert.

a. _____

b. _____

c. _____

2.037 Why is moisture like a blanket?

_____

_____

_____

✔	**Teacher check:**	Initials _____	80
	Score _____	Date _____	100

3. HOW DO PEOPLE LIVE IN THE DESERT?

Many people live in the desert. Before modern times their life was very hard. Even today many people live in traditional ways in the desert. They must search hard for food and water. They must try to stay cool in the hot desert days and warm at night.

In this section you will learn about traditional ways of life in the desert. You will also learn how man today has made the desert a comfortable place to live, using modern inventions and ideas.

Objectives

Read these objectives. When you have completed this section, you should be able to:

6. Describe the traditional ways of life in the desert.
7. Know the names and locations of some desert people.
8. Explain how modern inventions help people to live in the desert.

Vocabulary

Study these new words. Learning the meanings of these words is a good study habit and will improve your understanding of this LIFEPAC.

canal (kə nal′). Passage dug to carry water.

caravan (kar′ ə van). A group of travelers with their animals and goods.

climate (klī′ mit). The kind of weather a place most often has.

crop (krop). Plants grown or gathered by people for their use.

fertilizer (fėr′ təl ī zėr). A substance put into or on the soil to make it produce more.

gourd (gôrd). The fruit of a vine whose hard, dried shell is used for cups, bowls, and other utensils.

irrigation (ir′ə gā′ shən). Supplying land with water.

mine (mīn). A large hole dug in the earth to get out coal, salt, gold, or anything valuable.

modern (mod' ərn). Of the present time or times not long ago.

Muslim (mŭz' ləm, mŏŏz'-, mŭs'-, mŏŏs'-). A follower of the teachings of Islam; a religion started by a man named Muhammad.

nomads (nō' mad). A member of a tribe that moves from place to place to find food, or pasture for its animals.

ornament (ôr' nə mənt). Something that adds beauty.

sparse (spärs). Thinly scattered; occurring here and there.

traditional (trə dish' ə nəl). A way of behaving or living that is taught to children by their parents for many generations.

Pronunciation Key: h**a**t, **ã**ge, c**ã**re, f**ä**r; l**e**t, **ē**qual, t**ė**rm; **i**t, **ī**ce; h**o**t, **ō**pen, **ô**rder; **oi**l; **ou**t; c**u**p, p**u̇**t, r**ü**le; **ch**ild; lo**ng**; **th**in; /ͲH/ for **th**en; /zh/ for mea**s**ure; /u/ or /ə/ represents /a/ in **a**bout, /e/ in tak**e**n, /i/ in penc**i**l, /o/ in lem**o**n, and /u/ in circ**u**s.

Traditional Ways of Life

People who lived traditional lives in the desert can be divided into three groups. Hunter/gatherers lived by eating whatever they could find. **Nomads** lived by raising livestock and moving it to find food or water. Villagers built groups of homes and farms near sources of water and lived there. A few people still live traditional ways today.

Hunter/gatherers included the Aborigines of Australia and the Bushmen of the Kalahari and Namib Deserts. Nomads could be found in the Berbers of the Sahara, the Bedouins of Arabia, and the Mongols of the Gobi. Peoples who built villages near water sources included the Hopi and Navajo people of the American Southwest.

Hunter/gatherers. This group ate whatever food they could kill (hunt) or find (gather). Usually, the men did the hunting and the women did the gathering. They lived in small family groups that worked together to get food.

| Mesa Verde National Park

The groups moved from place to place looking for food. Wherever they camped, they put up a home of grass and sticks. When they moved on, they left the home behind. They would build new ones at the next camp.

Hunter/gatherers had to carry all of their things themselves. They had no animals to help, so they owned very little. They wore little or no clothing. A man might have his weapons and a few **ornaments**. A woman might have a digging stick, her ornaments, and a few hollow **gourds** to hold food or water.

Hunter/gatherers had to know their desert very well. They had to know where to find water, what plants could be eaten, where to find animals to hunt, and how to use everything they could find to help them live.

These people were very clever about using the things they found. The Bushmen in the Kalahari made water jugs out of hollow ostrich eggs and hunted with poison-tipped arrows. The Aborigines of Australia could find water in their desert far from the water holes. They knew how to find frogs that filled themselves up with water and hid in the ground. They would dig up the frogs and get water from them. These people used the minds God gave them to live in very difficult places.

Put the correct answer on each line.

3.1   Hunter/gatherers owned _____ .

3.2   The _____ usually did the hunting and the _____

did the gathering.

3.3   The three traditional ways of life in a desert were:

a. _____ , b. _____ ,

and c. _____ .

3.4   Hunter/gatherers built a new _____ every place they camped.

3.5   Hunter/gathers had to know their _____ very well to live there.

Berber and Bedouin nomads. The nomads of the Sahara and Arabian Deserts lived very much the same way. They lived in tents and raised livestock. They would travel from place to place to find food for their animals. They usually kept sheep, goats, cattle, camels, and perhaps horses. When the animals had eaten all the **sparse** grass in one place, the group packed up and moved to another.

Unlike hunter/gatherers, nomads had many possessions. They wore long, loose clothes which protected them from the sun. They lived in large tents. The desert under the tents was usually covered with rugs. Their horses and camels wore saddles that were often beautifully decorated. The men had metal weapons that were decorated. The women often owned lovely jewelry, metal cooking pots, and dishes. The nomads had camels to carry all of their things when they moved to a new place.

The nomads were able to trade meat, milk, and animal skins for fruit, vegetables, jewelry, pans, weapons, and other goods. They traded with the people who lived in villages on the larger oasis and with the traveling merchants who visited there.

The nomads also traded across the desert. Salt was very important and hard to find south of the Sahara Desert. However, there were huge salt plains in the northern Sahara where the rains had evaporated, and there were also salt **mines**. The nomads would take the salt across the desert in large **caravans** of camels. They often went to the city of Timbuktu, south of the Sahara, to trade their salt. The trade brought the nomads gold they could use to buy many beautiful things. In Arabia the nomads traded valuable resins called frankincense and myrrh which had to be taken across the desert.

The Berbers and Bedouins would fight fierce battles with each other over trade, use of oases, and insults made against their families. In one tribe, the Tuareg of the Sahara, the men wrapped long blue cloths

| Desert nomad

around their heads so that only their eyes showed. This made them look very fierce in battle. They would charge into battle on camels waving swords and spears.

These nomads all thought it was very important to be kind to visitors. They always offered food and drink. It was an insult to say no. These nomad people all became **Muslims** about 600 years after the birth of Jesus. At that time, large Muslim armies conquered the Arabian Peninsula and North Africa.

Mongol nomads. The nomads of the Gobi Desert also raised livestock to survive. The *steppes* grew enough grass to support large herds of goats, camels, yaks, sheep, cattle, and, most importantly, horses. The Mongol horses were small, tough animals, and the people were excellent riders.

The hard, flat steppes were great places to ride horses. The Mongols used horses to move their herds, just like cowboys. They used a rope on a long pole to catch any animal that tried to run away. They even learned to shoot a bow and arrow from the back of a running horse.

The Mongols did not trade like the Berbers and Bedouins. They had no nearby towns and villages to go to for trade. They got everything they needed from their animals. They ate mostly meat and milk. The milk was made into cheese, butter, yogurt, and a bubbly milk drink called *airag*. They made their clothes from the wool and skins of their animals. But, the most amazing thing they made was their homes.

A Mongol's home was a type of tent called a *ger* or *yurt*. It was built in a circle over a wood frame. The frame was built so it could be easily folded up. The frame was covered with felt. Felt is a cloth made by packing wool together very tightly. It is very thick and warm. These *gers* were good protection against the cold night weather of the Gobi Desert. Thus, nomad people were able to live in the deserts and have good lives there.

| A yurt

Put the correct answer on each line.

3.6 Nomads, unlike hunter/gatherers had many _____ .

3.7 The nomads of the Sahara were able to trade _____

across the desert using their camels.

3.8 Mongols got everything they need to live from their _____ .

3.9 The Mongols' most important animals were their _____ .

3.10 Berbers and Bedouins traded _____ , _____ , and

_____ for things they could not get from their animals.

Answer each question.

3.11 Why did nomads move from place to place?

_____

_____

_____

3.12 What did Berbers and Bedouins fight each other over?

_____

_____

_____

Match these items.

3.13	_____ Muslim	a.	Mongol's home
3.14	_____ *steppes*	b.	dry, flat plains
3.15	_____ caravan	c.	packed-down wool cloth
3.16	_____ made from milk	d.	cheese, butter, yogurt
3.17	_____ *ger*	e.	a group of traders traveling
3.18	_____ felt	f.	person who believes in Islam

Complete this activity.

3.19 Write a story about what it would be like for you to visit a nomad camp.

✔ **Teacher check:**

Initials _____   Date _____

Villagers. The village-building people of the American deserts grew **crops** along rivers and other sources of water. They grew food like corn, squash, and beans that did well in the dry **climate** and also gathered food from the desert plants. They kept small herds of sheep and hunted wild animals for food too. They used every source of food they could find. They had to do this because they did not use up all the food in one place and then move. They needed to always have enough food right near their village.

The Hopi people built their villages in an unusual place. They were built high on top of tall, straight-sided, flat-topped mountains called *mesas*. They did this to protect the village from attack. It would be difficult to attack the village if the enemies had to climb hundreds of feet up a cliff! The only problem was the Hopis had to climb down from the *mesa* each day to get water, take care of the crops, and tend the animals.

Hopi villages called pueblos were built like big apartment houses, one on top of the other. They were made of blocks of sun-dried mud called adobe (ə dō′ bē) bricks. The adobe bricks were built into thick walls which kept them cool during the day and warm at night.

Navajo (nav′ ə hō) villages were built on the flat desert. Their homes were made of logs covered with dirt. They were called *hogans*. Again, the thick walls protected the people from the heat and cold of the desert.

| Navajo hogan

Navajo and Hopi people made all the things they needed to live. They shaped clay into pots or jars and baked it to make pottery. They wove baskets from the leaves of desert plants. They wove clothes and blankets from the wool of their sheep. They also learned how to make their things very beautiful by weaving designs and painting the pottery. Today some of these people still do the traditional crafts. The baskets, pottery, and blankets are expensive to buy because they take so long to make and are so beautiful.

Answer *true* or *false*.

3.20 _____ Hopi people built their homes on the desert floor.

3.21 _____ A *hogan* is a Navajo home.

3.22 _____ Village people grew crops and raised animals.

3.23 _____ Village people used all the food in one spot and then moved someplace else.

3.24 _____ A pueblo is a Hopi village.

3.25 _____ Hopi and Navajo people made beautiful blankets, baskets, and pottery.

Modern Ways of Life

Modern machines and knowledge have made the desert a more comfortable place to live. People have found good ways to bring large amounts of water into the desert. Farmers have learned how to make the best use of the water to grow food in the desert.

There are big cities in the desert today. The water allows many people to live there. Other inventions, like air conditioning, make life comfortable in the desert. People have learned to be creative in finding ways to live in the desert today.

One way to bring water to the desert is to build **canals**. These long ditches and/or pipes bring water from a large lake or river across the desert. With today's modern equipment, the water can come from a long way. The Central Arizona Project, for example, is a 336-mile long system of pipes and canals that brings water to Phoenix, Arizona in the Sonoran Desert.

Another way to bring in water is to put up a dam across the rivers that come into the desert. The lake behind the dam becomes a big water tank. The short, heavy desert rainfall can be kept until it is needed in drier times.

Another way is to use modern equipment to dig deep wells. These wells can reach water far underground, then an electric pump can bring the water up for people to use.

Farmers can grow food in the desert by using **irrigation**. The water is pumped into long, shallow trenches beside the growing plants, so their roots can reach it. However, the water evaporates and leaves salt behind that will kill the crops, so the farmer has to use a large amount of water to wash away the salt. He also has to use fertilizer to make the barren desert soil right for growing crops.

Some farms use very special ways to grow food in the desert. One way is called hydroponics. In *hydroponics*, the farmer grows the crops inside a large building without using any dirt. The plants are hung from string, with their roots in a nutrient liquid that makes them grow. Very little water is lost to evaporation because the plants are inside, protected from the desert sun and dry air.

| Hoover Dam, Arizona

Complete these activities.

3.26 List three ways to bring water to a desert.

a. _____

b. _____

c. _____

3.27 Farmers can grow food in the desert using _____ to water the plants.

3.28 A special kind of indoor farming that uses no dirt is called

_____ .

3.29 The Central Arizona Project brings water to

_____ .

Other modern inventions make life more comfortable in the desert. Air conditioning allows people inside to be cool and comfortable even when it is 115°F outside. Modern roads and cars allow people to travel quickly and easily across the desert. They also allow food to be brought in easily from non-desert areas. Airplanes can even bring in food from the other side of the world!

When a city is built in the desert, the people must build their homes for life in the desert. Houses are built with walls that keep out the heat. Window screens are made so that they shade the window from the sun. Houses are painted light colors that reflect the sunlight away from the house. Yards are filled with desert plants and watered by small pipes that drip right on the roots. Cars use reflective film on some of their windows to block out the sun.

The desert has one very important source of electric power—sunlight. Solar panels create electricity from sunlight. It takes quite a bit of sunlight for them to work, and each module does not make a great deal of electricity but many of them together in a large panel do a good job. They work very well in the desert, though, and larger sets of panels can add electricity to the distribution lines.

Some people have done very creative things to live in the desert. In Australia, many people make their living by raising sheep on desert grasslands. It takes a large piece of land to raise the sheep, so the people live far apart. The children go to school by radio! If someone needs a doctor, he comes by airplane. On the Arabian Peninsula, fresh water is made by using huge factories that take the salt out of the nearby ocean water.

| Solar panels in Egypt

One very clever idea allows people who live along the coast in the Atacama Desert to "harvest the clouds," the fog that comes in but never drops rain. They put up plastic sheets or nets on the mountains above their homes, with pans underneath them. The plastic catches the moisture in the fog and forms drops of water. The water drops fall into the pans, which drain into pipes. The pipes carry the water down to the people below. It is all very simple and costs very little to build.

If you ever visit the town of Coober Pedy, Australia, you might have trouble finding it. Most of the town is underground! The houses, stores, restaurants, and even hotels are built that way to stay cool in the hot desert. This is another clever way people live in the desert.

Even today people who live in deserts must be careful. Deserts are hard places for people. When they go outside, people must use sunscreen to prevent sunburn. They wear sunglasses and hats to protect their eyes and face from the sun. They have to drink extra water in the dry, hot air. If they work outside, they must be careful not to do too much or they will get sick. Hiking out into the desert without enough water is dangerous. A few people die every year in the American deserts making that mistake.

Deserts are hard places for plants, animals, and people to live. The plants and animals were specially created by God to live in such a dry, hot place. God gave men brains, so they could find ways to live in the desert themselves. Men used the minds God gave them to live in the desert long ago. Modern people have learned how to live in the desert comfortably, using new machines and clever ideas, but desert life will always be hard on plants, animals, and people.

Answer each question.

3.30   Why do these inventions make life in the desert easier?

a. air conditioning _____

_____

b. roads and cars _____

_____

3.31   What is the one important source of electric power in the desert?

_____

3.32   How do the people in the Atacama Desert "harvest the clouds"?

_____

_____

_____

_____

Circle the correct word.

3.33   Coober Pedy, Australia is (underwater / underground / on a cliff).

3.34   Solar panels create electricity from (water / air / sunlight).

3.35   Deserts are (hard / easy / impossible) places for plants, animals, and people to live.

3.36   Hiking in the desert without enough (food / water / toys) is dangerous.

3.37   Children who live spread out on the desert in Australia go to school by (bus / train / radio).

3.38   In desert cities, houses are (light colors / dark colors).

Complete this activity.

3.39 Draw a picture of Coober Pedy, Australia.

Teacher check:

Initials _____ Date _____

Before you take this last Self Test, you may want to do one or more of these self checks.

1. _____ Read the objectives. See if you can do them.
2. _____ Restudy the material related to any objectives that you cannot do.
3. _____ Use the **SQ3R** study procedure to review the material:
    a. **S**can the sections.
    b. **Q**uestion yourself.
    c. **R**ead to answer your questions.
    d. **R**ecite the answers to yourself.
    e. **R**eview areas you did not understand.
4. _____ Review all vocabulary, activities, and Self Tests, writing a correct answer for every wrong answer.

SELF TEST 3

Match these items by writing the correct letter on the line (2 points each answer).

3.01 _____ kangaroo rat

3.02 _____ hydroponics

3.03 _____ camel

3.04 _____ ger

3.05 _____ aquifer

3.06 _____ dune

3.07 _____ irrigation

3.08 _____ date palm

3.09 _____ hunter/gatherers

3.10 _____ nomads

3.11 _____ villagers

3.12 _____ felt

3.13 _____ salt

3.14 _____ solar panels

3.15 _____ caravan

3.16 _____ pottery, baskets

a. a Mongol nomad's home

b. pile of sand blown by the wind

c. traditional desert people who plant crops and do not move

d. raising crop indoors without dirt in a special liquid

e. pressed-down wool cloth

f. item traded by Sahara nomads

g. "ship of the desert"

h. makes electricity from sunlight

i. a group of traveling traders

j. traditional Hopi and Navajo crafts

k. large area of underground water

l. supplying land with water

m. traditional desert people who raise livestock and move to find food

n. desert plant that produces fruit, leaves for mats, wood for fuel

o. traditional desert people who eat what they can kill or find

p. animal, eats seeds and plants, needs no water

Name the continent where each desert is found. Some answers will be used twice (3 points each answer).

3.017 Sahara _____

3.018 Atacama _____

3.019 American Southwest _____

3.020 Kalahari _____

3.021 Arabian _____

3.022 Gobi _____

3.023 Australian _____

Choose the correct word to complete each sentence (3 points each answer).

Capricorn	Cancer	Berber
Mongol	pueblos	hemisphere

3.024 The line of dry area north of the equator is the Tropic of

_____ .

3.025 The line of dry area south of the equator is the Tropic of

_____ .

3.026 The nomads of the Gobi Desert who raised horses on the *steppes* were called

_____ .

3.027 The nomads of the Sahara Desert who became Muslims were the

_____ .

3.028 One half of the earth is called a _____ .

3.029 Hopi villages, built on top of *mesas*, were called _____ .

Answer each question (5 points each answer).

3.030   How do the people of the Atacama Desert "harvest the clouds"?

_____

_____

_____

_____

3.031   What are the two ways moisture can be blocked from reaching a desert?

a. _____

b. _____

3.032   Why are lakes in a desert often salty?

_____

_____

_____

Answer _true_ or _false_ (1 point each answer).

3.033   _____   Hunter/gatherers do not own many things.

3.034   _____   Nomads do not own many things.

3.035   _____   Digging wells is one way to bring water into a desert.

3.036   _____   Desert animals usually hunt for food at night when it is cooler.

3.037   _____   Cactus have insides like a sponge to fill with water after it rains.

3.038   _____   Desert plants can only live near a lake or river.

3.039   _____   It is safe to hike in the desert without extra water.

3.040   _____   There are no deserts in Europe.

3.041   _____   The Nile River is in the Sahara Desert.

Teacher check: Initials _____
Score _____   Date _____

80 / 100

Before you take the LIFEPAC Test, you may want to do one or more of these self checks.

1. _____ Read the objectives. See if you can do them.
2. _____ Restudy the material related to any objectives that you cannot do.
3. _____ Use the **SQ3R** study procedure to review the material.
4. _____ Review activities, Self Tests, and LIFEPAC vocabulary words.
5. _____ Restudy areas of weakness indicated by the last Self Test.

NOTES

NOTES